LIGHT the CANDLE! BANG the DRUM!

A book of holidays around the world

BY **Ann Morris**

PICTURES BY **Peter Linenthal**

Dutton Children's Books
NEW YORK

For my mother, Alice, with much love

P.A.L.

Text copyright © 1997 by Ann Morris
Illustrations copyright © 1997 by Peter Linenthal

Library of Congress Cataloging-in-Publication Data

Morris, Ann, date.
Light the candle! bang the drum!: a book of holidays from around the world
by Ann Morris; illustrated by Peter Linenthal.
p. cm.
Summary: Illustrations and brief text present various holidays celebrated
around the world, including New Year's Day, Presidents' Day, Easter,
Diwali, Posadas, and Hanukkah.
ISBN 0-525-45639-2 (hc)
1. Holidays—Juvenile literature. [1. Holidays.] I. Linenthal, Peter, ill. II. Title.
GT3933.M65 1997 394.26—dc21 97-5373 CIP AC

Published in the United States 1997 by Dutton Children's Books,
a division of Penguin Books USA Inc.
375 Hudson Street, New York, New York 10014
Designed by Amy Berniker
Printed in Hong Kong   First Edition
10 9 8 7 6 5 4 3 2 1

NEW YEAR'S DAY

Good-bye, old year! At midnight,
a new year begins. Horns blow.
People throw confetti. Everyone
shouts: "Happy New Year!"

MARTIN LUTHER KiNG, JR., DAY

Martin Luther King, Jr., wanted people of all races to love and respect one another. We celebrate his life and dreams for a better world.

A new moon signals the new year. Red candles burn, and children get good-luck gifts in red paper. Firecrackers scare away the bad spirits.

LUNAR NEW YEAR

VALENTINE'S DAY

Make a card with hearts and flowers
and give it to the one you love.
Will you be my valentine?

PRESIDENTS' DAY

Two great American leaders—George Washington and Abraham Lincoln— were born in February. We honor them and all they did for our country.

CARNIVAL

Everyone is in masks and costumes. There is singing and dancing and lots of noise in the street. Come join the parade!

ST. PATRICK'S DAY

Shamrocks are everywhere! The whole town turns green and dances a jig to celebrate with the Irish!

EASTER

The Easter bunny brings brightly colored eggs that we hunt for in the grass. Put them in your basket and celebrate the arrival of spring.

MAY DAY

Spring is here at last. To celebrate, people gather flowers. In the town square, they dance around the maypole with ribbons in their hands.

CHILDREN'S DAY

Kites in the shape of fish wave over rooftops. They are meant to show strength and courage. Elders wish the children health and happiness.

The corn is ripe. Native Americans give thanks at a big feast. There is eating, singing, and dancing throughout the day.

GREEN CORN FESTIVAL

Prayers and fasting are over.
Families dress in new clothes
and visit friends, bringing sweets,
flowers, and presents.

EID AL-FITR

Parades, waving flags, fireworks! It's Independence Day in the United States—the day when freedom first rang in our land.

Children dressed as witches, goblins, and spooky ghosts yell, "Trick or Treat!" Pumpkins are carved to look like scary faces. *Boo!*

DiWALi

Diwali means "row of lights." Floors are painted with bright-colored powders. Twinkling lights everywhere mark the new year.

Rattle, rattle! Skeletons shake their bones and bang their drums. We remember relatives and friends who have died, and we celebrate life.

DAY OF THE DEAD

Little boats, each with a candle and a wish, float down the river. Overhead, fireworks light their way under the full moon.

LOY KRATHONG

THANKSGIVING

We help ourselves to all we can eat.
We give thanks for what we have.
And we think of the Pilgrims and the
Native Americans of long ago.

HANUKKAH

Light the menorah! Spin the dreidel! Families come together to sing, laugh, eat latkes—and remember the flame that burned for eight nights.

ST. LUCIA'S DAY

The daughter of the house wears
a crown with seven candles.
She brings sweet buns and
light in the early morning.

POSADAS

Children dressed as Joseph and Mary go from house to house. At last they find a place to stay. Then the piñata is broken, and out pours the candy.

Brrrr! Snow is falling. Skiers fly by. *Clop clop* go the three horses pulling the sled. Sleigh bells ring to welcome Grandfather Frost and the New Year.

RUSSIAN WINTER FESTIVAL

CHRISTMAS

Merry Christmas! It's time to trim the tree and make cookies and sweets. People sing carols and exchange presents at this joyful time.

KWANZAA

For seven days, African-Americans celebrate their history and customs. Families gather and rejoice in the seven symbols of the holiday.

NOTES

New Year's Day (Worldwide) JANUARY 1
All over the world, people who use the Roman calendar celebrate the arrival of the new year on the first of January. The night before, New Year's Eve, is often a time for parties and for making New Year's resolutions. As the clock strikes midnight, people sing, shout, make noise, offer a toast, and wish each other a Happy New Year.

Martin Luther King, Jr., Day (USA) OBSERVED ON THE THIRD MONDAY IN JANUARY
Dr. Martin Luther King, Jr., was a preacher and a great champion of freedom and civil rights. He believed that all races, religions, and nationalities should work together to make a better world. He fought poverty and racial discrimination, and believed that change could happen peacefully. To keep his memory alive and to remind us of the ideals for which he died, the United States Congress has honored him by making his birthday a national holiday. He is the first African-American to be honored in this way.

Lunar New Year (China, Vietnam, Korea, Southeast Asia) OBSERVED ON THE FIRST DAY OF THE FIRST MOON IN JANUARY OR FEBRUARY
This holiday, which comes in January or February, celebrates the new year according to the Chinese calendar and the beginning of spring in China. People clean their homes and sweep away the old year. They light red candles and put up red decorations, which are thought to bring good luck. For the new year, children receive little red envelopes of "lucky money" to buy holiday treats and gifts. People set off firecrackers and march in parades, carrying large silk dragons, symbols of strength and good luck.

Valentine's Day (Canada, Europe, USA) FEBRUARY 14
This day is a special celebration of love and friendship, and is symbolized by the heart. No one is sure how Valentine's Day and the custom of exchanging gifts and cards began, but by the seventeenth century it became the custom to send a greeting card to someone you love. Today, people give cards as well as candy and flowers. Many children make their own cards with poems and messages to celebrate the holiday.

Presidents' Day (USA) OBSERVED ON THE THIRD MONDAY IN FEBRUARY
Americans celebrate the combined birthdays of Abraham Lincoln and George Washington, two of the country's greatest presidents, on a single day. Washington was the commander in chief of the American army in the Revolutionary War. He led the fledgling country to independence from the British and was elected the first president of the United States. Abraham Lincoln led the United States through the Civil War, which divided the North and the South. He issued the Emancipation Proclamation, which outlawed slavery in the South.

Carnival (Christian—Brazil; France; Italy; Germany; New Orleans, USA) OBSERVED IN FEBRUARY OR MARCH, THE DAY BEFORE LENT
Carnival is celebrated on the last day before the start of Lent, the time before Easter when many Christians give up meat. Formerly, people also gave up butter and eggs, and it was the tradition to use up the last of these ingredients to make pancakes. The day when they do this is called Mardi Gras—French for "Fat Tuesday"—the last chance to have fun before the long Lenten season begins. There are balls and costume parties. In Brazil, Carnival is a very important holiday, and people parade through the streets wearing elaborate costumes and dancing the samba.

St. Patrick's Day (Ireland, USA) MARCH 17
St. Patrick's Day honors the saint who spread the Christian faith in Ireland in the fourth century. He used the green shamrock with its three leaves to explain the Trinity—the idea that God, Jesus, and the Holy Spirit are one. Today, people of Irish heritage celebrate the day with parades and "the wearing of the green."

Easter (Christian) OBSERVED ON THE SUNDAY FOLLOWING THE FIRST FULL MOON AFTER THE VERNAL EQUINOX; MAY FALL FROM MARCH 22 TO APRIL 25
The spring festival of Easter is the most important day of the Christian year, celebrating the day Jesus ascended into heaven. Because this springtime holiday symbolizes renewal, rebirth, and fertility, eggs and rabbits are associated with it. Coloring eggs began with medieval travelers returning from Egypt and Persia, and it is the custom for the Easter bunny to bring brightly decorated eggs to children. On Easter Sunday, many people dress up in their best clothes and fancy hats for church, and may go strolling in the Easter Parade.

May Day (Worldwide) MAY 1
May Day has its roots in ancient Rome, where people honored Flora, the goddess of springtime, by carrying flowers to her temple. In medieval northern Europe, all classes of people awoke at dawn on the first of May to go "a-Maying." In a long parade, they carried trees and garlands of green branches and flowers to the town square. The Maypole formed the center of the procession and was decorated with wreaths and ribbons, which people held as they walked or danced around the pole. May Day also became known as a holiday for working people, and in many countries it continues to be celebrated as a labor day.

Children's Day (Japan) MAY 5
Once called Boys' Day, Children's Day now celebrates all children. Each child in the household traditionally flies a kite in the shape of a carp—a symbol of strength, courage, and determination. In Shinto shrines, priests wave white streamers overhead, blessing the people and wishing them happiness.

Green Corn Festival (Northeast and Southeast USA) JULY
For four days, Native Americans of the Iroquois, Seminole, Choctaw, and Cherokee tribes celebrate the new corn crop. They feast, dance, and play games. After a sacred ceremony, everyone dances the Green Corn Dance with feathers, fans, rattles, and a water drum. They give prayers of thanks to the Creator for the harvest and enjoy feasting on corn soup, corn bread, corn pudding, and corn on the cob.

Eid al-Fitr (Muslim) OBSERVED THE FIRST DAY OF THE TENTH MONTH OF THE ISLAMIC CALENDAR
Eid al-Fitr marks the end of the month-long fast of Ramadan. *Eid* means "a festival of happiness—a great time of joy," and celebrates when God sent down the Koran, the Muslim holy book. People give special prayers of thanksgiving to God for their faith and for giving them the Koran. It is a time to forgive as well as to celebrate. Families visit with one another and feast on meat and rice dishes.

Fourth of July — Independence Day (USA) JULY 4
This day is celebrated as the birthday of the United States of America. In 1776, representatives of twelve of the thirteen British colonies in America approved the final draft

of the Declaration of Independence, written by Thomas Jefferson, proclaiming the country free from British rule and asserting that "all men created equal." After it was read, the Liberty Bell was rung in Philadelphia. Today, every town in the United States celebrates with parades, band concerts, family picnics, and fireworks.

Halloween (USA, Canada, Ireland, Great Britain) OCTOBER 31

Halloween is a very old custom. At the harvest festival at the beginning of winter, people used to honor the dead. In the ninth century, the Catholic Church created a holiday for remembering all the saints, All Hallows' Eve, which eventually became Halloween. But people still associated this day with the spirits of all the dead, and they wore masks and costumes and told ghost stories to scare the spirits away, and lit bonfires intended to ward them off. Pumpkins, an autumn vegetable, were cut and made into jack-o'-lanterns, brightly lit with a candle inside.

Diwali (Hindu—India, Pakistan) OBSERVED IN OCTOBER OR NOVEMBER OF THE HINDU CALENDAR

Diwali, the festival of lights, is a celebration of the new year. People clean their homes and decorate the floors with colored rice powder in beautiful designs to welcome Lakshmi, the Hindu goddess of prosperity. Thousands of sparklers and twinkling lamps are put on paths and rooftops to help light her way. Children put candlewicks in tiny clay saucers filled with mustard-seed oil.

Day of the Dead — El Día de Los Muertos (Mexico) OBSERVED ON NOVEMBER 1 AND/OR 2 IN COMMEMORATION OF ALL SAINTS' DAY AND ALL SOULS' DAY

This holiday honors friends and relatives who have died, but it is also a time to celebrate life and unite to mock death. Stores sell painted skeletons, sweet bread shaped like human skulls and bones (called *pan de los muertos*), and ghosts, skeletons, and skulls made of candies. Families visit cemeteries and set up altars at home with pictures of relatives who have died. They stock their houses with food to feed the ghosts. People dressed as skeletons dance in the streets among bursting firecrackers.

Loy Krathong (Thailand) OBSERVED ON THE DAY OF THE FULL MOON OF THE TWELFTH LUNAR MONTH

The meaning of Loy Krathong can be found in its name. *Loy* means "to float," and *krathong* means "leaf." During the festival, children sail little banana-leaf *krathongs* down the river. These are filled with flowers and a candle. The legend is that if the light from the candle lasts until the *krathong* disappears from sight, the child's wish will come true.

Thanksgiving (USA) OBSERVED ON THE FOURTH THURSDAY IN NOVEMBER

Thanksgiving is a harvest festival that is celebrated by different nationalities and religions in the United States. It commemorates the time when Squanto, a Pawtuxet Indian later associated with the Wampanoag tribe, helped the colonists at Plymouth with their crops. At harvest time, the colony held a celebration and invited Massasoit, the chief of the tribe, to join their feast of turkey, venison, duck, goose, lobsters, clams, corn, vegetables, and dried berries. Today, families come together to give thanks for all they have and to enjoy a traditional feast of turkey, cranberry sauce, sweet potatoes, and pumpkin pie.

Hanukkah (Jewish) OBSERVED IN NOVEMBER OR DECEMBER

When the Syrians occupied Jerusalem thousands of years ago, Judah Maccabee led a rebellion to free his people so they could worship their own God. To celebrate their victory and to rededicate the Temple, the Maccabees proclaimed an eight-day festival. However, they had only enough oil to light their lamp for one day. A miracle took place, and the oil lasted eight days. Hanukkah, the festival of lights, celebrates this miracle and the rededication of the Temple. On Hanukkah, Jewish people celebrate for eight nights, lighting candles on the menorah, spinning the dreidel, and exchanging gifts.

St. Lucia's Day (Italy, Sweden, Norway) OBSERVED IN DECEMBER ON THE DAY OF THE WINTER SOLSTICE

St. Lucia was born in Italy. Her name means "light," and in Scandinavia she has become a symbol of hope and the promise of spring at the darkest time of the year. In Sweden, a feast is held on the winter solstice—the shortest day of the year. In the morning, the oldest daughter of the family dresses in a long white robe with a wreath of candles on her head and serves saffron buns and coffee. The younger boys wear long, pointed hats with stars and act as her attendants.

Posadas — The Inns (Mexico) DECEMBER 16—23

On the eight nights before the Christmas celebration, Mexican children dress up as Mary and Joseph and reenact their search for shelter on the night that Jesus was born. Crowds follow Mary and Joseph to different houses until, at the ninth house, they are let in. At the party there, children try to break a piñata with a stick and then eat the candies that fall from it.

Russian Winter Festival (Russia) DECEMBER—JANUARY 5

During Russian Winter Festival, shops display bright lights, snowmen, and decorations to welcome patrons who buy gifts to exchange on New Year's Eve. Children wait for Grandfather Frost and his helper, Snow Girl, who give presents and wish everyone Happy New Year. Children skate, ski, and follow the traditional custom of riding sleighs that are pulled across the snow by troikas, three-horse teams.

Christmas (Christian) DECEMBER 25

Christmas celebrates the birth of the baby Jesus. On this most festive and joyous holiday, people go to church, sing carols, and exchange gifts with family and friends. With its candles and burning Yule log, this holiday is also a celebration of the return of the sun in the middle of winter.

Kwanzaa (USA) DECEMBER

Kwanzaa, a celebration of unity, was first celebrated in 1966 by African-American teacher Dr. Maulana Karenga so that African-Americans could learn about and honor their history and customs. *Kwanzaa* means "first fruits of the harvest" in Swahili. People spend time together and welcome one another into their homes. They light one candle for each of seven days on a candleholder called a *kinara*. There is an ear of corn for every child in the family. They share food and exchange family stories and presents.

and your own special day...

YOUR BiRTHDAY!